Spiritual Lessons from Dartmoor Forest

GW00371972

By the Rev. H. HUGH BRETON, M.A.

FOREST PUBLISHING

First published 1929 (Part I), 1930 (Part II)
Republished in facsimile (combined edition) in 1990 by FOREST
PUBLISHING, Woodstock, Liverton, Newton Abbot, Devon TQ12 6JJ.

British Library Cataloguing in Publication Data
Breton, Henry Hugh b. 1873
    Spiritual Lessons from Dartmoor Forest.
    1.   Christian life. Devotional works
    I.   Title
    242

ISBN 0-9515274-2-8

Forest Publishing

Sales and distribution by:
Town & Country Books
P.O. Box 31, Newton Abbot, Devon TQ12 5XH.

Editorial, design and colour photography by:
Mike and Roger Lang.

Typeset by:
Exe Valley Dataset Ltd, Exeter.

Printed and bound in Great Britain by:
BPCC Wheatons Ltd, Exeter.

CONTENTS

Introduction

Part I—"White Heather" and other studies

Part II—"Crystal Streams" and other studies

Appendices

This single volume is a complete facsimile of the original two-part work and includes all of the text from those works.

The Reverend Henry Hugh Breton, M.A.

INTRODUCTION TO
THE FACSIMILE EDITION

HENRY HUGH BRETON was born in Southampton on 16 September 1873 and was educated at Southampton Boys' College.

Shortly after leaving school he decided on ordination in the Church of England and was admitted as a Pensioner (the second of the three ranks in which students were matriculated) to Christ's College, Cambridge on 1 October 1892, prior to being formally admitted as a student in the University at Michaelmas, 1892.

In 1895 he obtained a Bachelor of Arts degree and entered Wells Theological College. Then, during the following year, he was ordained as a deacon—he was to be ordained as a priest (at Chichester) in 1897—and began his ministry as Curate of Christ Church, Blacklands, Hastings and was also Assistant Chaplain of Hastings Borough Cemetery. During his time here he obtained a Master of Arts degree (1899) and married his childhood sweetheart, Mabel Pennington Gorringe.

On 1 November 1907 he took up the living of Sheepstor, Devon which, in 1921, merged with Meavy to become Meavy with Sheepstor. He then exchanged for Alfriston, Sussex in the following year (1922) until vacating the benefice there on 1 August 1923.

Two months later, on 1 October 1923, he became incumbent at Morwenstow, Cornwall, an area previously renowned for smuggling and ship-wrecks. It was also an area immortalised by the Reverend Robert Stephen Hawker, a genuine eccentric, a natural wit and a poet and author. He had been vicar there from 1834 until his death in 1875 and amongst other great works of his was the origination, in 1843, of the Harvest Festival.

From there Hugh Breton moved to become incumbent at Dean Prior, Devon, on 21 May 1927, where, once again, he had a well-known predecessor. On this occasion it was the Devon Poet-vicar, Robert Herrick, who had been vicar of the Church from 1629 until 1674.

His last appointment was as Rector of Meshaw with Creacombe, Devon where he became incumbent on 29 May 1931 until vacating the benefice on 30 June 1933, when ill-health forced him to bring forward his retirement. He then moved to

Westham, Sussex (the home of both his and his wife's ancestors) where he lived until his death on 13 September 1936, and lies buried, with his wife, who died just over four years later, in the Churchyard of St Mary's Parish Church, Westham.

In addition to his pastoral duties, Hugh Breton was well known for his work with the Meteorological Office in London and during his life-time became a Fellow of the Royal Meteorological Society.

———

Having spoken to a number of his former parishioners (to whom I should like to take this opportunity of expressing my sincere thanks), I can state with some authority that throughout his life Hugh Breton (and his wife) was both well-liked and highly respected. He also had a great sense of humour and one particular story that has been related to me illustrates this aspect only too well . . .

Whilst Vicar of Dean Prior he took great delight in telling his (amused) congregation during a Church Service about a certain prelate who, in the earlier years of his ministerial life, had asked a North Country farmer for an opinion as to how he was regarded by the Parishioners and been told "Well sir, we'll summer you and we'll winter you and then we'll tell you what we think of you".

Although I have received varying comments on the subject, it appears that he was at least partially deaf and had a slight speech impediment. One particular account concerning his speech, which was the source of some amusement to one of his former parishioners (a young lad at the time), was his inability to pronounce his "Rs" with the result that during Church services "Let us pray" would sound like "Let us pay"!

A quality of the man was his kind and good-hearted nature. He would give parties at the various vicarages for the Church choir and bell-ringers, was particularly sensitive to the needs of the children of the parishes in which he served (he had no children of his own), especially at Christmas time, and was always willing and prepared to take positive measures to raise money for charitable causes, one of which prompted him to write his first book . . .

———

Even before taking up his appointment at Sheepstor it is quite apparent that Hugh Breton had already grown to love Dartmoor (see Chapter I of The Beautiful Dartmoor Series—No. 1). However, whereas previous excursions appear to have been mainly superficial he now began to explore the Moor in depth, kept copious notes and made a good number of friends with such notables as Robert Burnard, Richard Hansford Worth and Sabine Baring-Gould (the Squire and Rector of Lewtrenchard). Before long he also became an active member of the Dartmoor Preservation Association, playing an important role in the restoration of various ancient monuments and Dartmoor crosses, particularly within the Sheepstor parish.

As his knowledge of the Moor increased, and as a means of raising money towards a fund set up for the restoration of the Rood Screen at Sheepstor Church, he then embarked on his first book, which gave birth to "The Beautiful Dartmoor Series" (originally called "The Sheepstor Series") in 1911. In all, five volumes were published—two more on Dartmoor and another two on Cornwall—and so successful were they that all were subsequently reprinted, the first volume reaching its fourth edition. This, in turn, enabled some of the profits to be subsequently channelled into a new fund for re-seating Sheepstor Church with oak seats incorporating finely carved bench-ends.

Later, on becoming incumbent at Morwenstow, Hugh Breton returned to his writing activities and produced four more books under the collective name of "The Morwenstow Series of Shilling Books", the intention on this occasion being to direct the profits to the Church Restoration Fund. Whilst at Morwenstow he also raised money for the erection of a granite cross to Cornish design in memory of the mariners who lay buried there, besides holding two particularly memorable services (on 11 August 1924 and 5 August 1925) on the Atlantic shore at Duck Pool, which were called "Blessing the Sea". The reasons were three-fold:

1. "To invoke God's blessing on the sea, on the ships which navigate the sea, on the thousands of brave men who man the ships, both in the Royal Navy and in the mercantile marine".
2. "To pray for the fruits of the sea on which we are so dependent for our food supply".
3. "To remember before God those who have been drowned in the sea, especially those whose mortal remains have been washed ashore on the coast line of the parish of Morwenstow".

After vacating the benefice of Morwenstow, Hugh Breton went on to write no less than eight more books between 1928 and 1932, and once again devoted the profits to Church work, on this occasion part to an Improvements Fund of Meshaw Church and the other part to a fund for re-hanging the bells at Dean Prior. The titles included "Spiritual Lessons from Dartmoor Forest" (in two parts), "The Word Pictures of the Bible" (also in two parts), "The Great Blizzard of Christmas, 1927" and "The Great Winter of 1928–29". The final two were part of a projected series entitled "The Forest of Dartmoor" covering the South-east, South-west, North-east and North-west quarters of the Moor which, unfortunately, was never completed due to failing health. Furthermore, all attempts made to obtain any manuscripts, partially completed or otherwise, in connection with the second two parts of this series and also other projected titles prior to his death have failed. Instead, it appears that if there ever were any they have been destroyed.

MIKE LANG
January 1990

Part 1

"White Heather"

and other studies

𝔖𝔭𝔦𝔯𝔦𝔱𝔲𝔞𝔩 𝔏𝔢𝔰𝔰𝔬𝔫𝔰

from

𝔇𝔞𝔯𝔱𝔪𝔬𝔬𝔯 𝔉𝔬𝔯𝔢𝔰𝔱

Part 1.

"White Heather" and other studies.

By the Rev. H. HUGH BRETON, M.A.

Author of "Beautiful Dartmoor," "The Breezy Cornish Moors,"
"Land's End and The Lizard," "The North Coast of Cornwall,"
"Morwenstow," "Hawker of Morwenstow," "The Heart of
Dartmoor," "The Word Pictures of the Bible," &c.

PRICE 1/-   Postage 1½d.

" In the shade, but shining ;
Reflecting the Light, that shineth
more and more unto the Perfect Day."

ENTERED AT STATIONERS' HALL.

Spiritual Lessons

from

Dartmoor Forest

Part 1.

"WHITE HEATHER" and other studies.

___

By the Rev. H. HUGH BRETON, M.A.

Author of ' Beautiful Dartmoor,' 'The Breezy Cornish
Moors," " Lands End and The Lizard," " The North
Coast of Cornwall," " Morwenstow," " Hawker of
Morwenstow,' ' The Heart of Dartmoor,' ' The Word
Pictures of The Bible," &c,

___

Price 1/-   Postage 1½d.

___

PRINTED & PUBLISHED BY
HOYTEN & COLE,
39, WHIMPLE STREET, PLYMOUTH.
1929.

PREFACE.

THESE little meditations are rough-shaped like the granite boulders which strew the slopes of the Dartmoor mountains. I hope they may appeal to lovers of Dartmoor and be a little help and refreshment to them, to soul as well as body.

Nature has many spiritual lessons to teach those who have the spiritual eye to see and the spiritual mind to learn.

The illustrations are not drawn from the imagination, but from actual observations of nature, which is ever ready to convey spiritual lessons to a spiritual man.

If this little volume is acceptable and helpful to my readers, several other parts will follow. It has a bright little companion—"The Word Pictures of the New Testament," Part I., "Some Aspects of Life," now ready.

H. HUGH BRETON.

DEAN PRIOR VICARAGE,
    June 1*st*, 1929.

WHITE HEATHER

The white flower of a blameless life.

ONE of the delights of the Dartmoor wanderer over the purple hills in summer or early autumn, is to find a sprig of white heather.

Just before I began building the Rood Screen at Sheepstor, the Rev. S. Baring-Gould was spending a day with me, and we were walking across the purple heather on Ringmoor Down. I spied in the distance a bunch of white heather, and I picked it and brought him some. He said " *Now* you will get your Screen "—and I did.

These are features about white heather which resemble a really good life :

(i) *Its rarity*. One may walk all day across the heather moors and not find a scrap. It is often as rare as the white flower of a blameless life.

(ii) *It grows in clusters*. Many years ago there lived a family near Dorchester ; at its head was a noble father, and a saintly mother. They had several sons, and the saintly mother always prayed daily that her sons might all grow up to be good men, and live useful lives in God's service. After the mother was gone, two became Bishops, two Archdeacons, and another lived a most useful life and benefited his generation; here the blameless lives grew in a cluster. So sometimes in a parish we find quite an assembly of good men and women.

(iii) *It stands out boldly in its purple setting*. So a really saintly life stands out conspicuously in its environment. The world in which it is placed is dark and forbidding ; standing up in this setting is the white flower of a blameless life.

THE BEARDOWN MAN

ON the high ground above the West Dart, a few yards N. of Devil Tor, stands the Beardown Man, a lonely Menhir commanding a remarkable view of the desert; all around are vast solitudes. This menhir marks the site of the grave of some chieftain of prehistoric days, whose friends and retainers chose this solitary resting-place for his mortal remains.

Standing as it does, so conspicuously, commanding the plain, it proclaims to a silent world the solitude of the death, as far as earthly companionship is concerned.

This is the one journey which we have to make alone ; we have our earthly friends with us up to the last moment; then when the severance comes we set out alone on the journey, but Christ meets us on the threshold of the Unseen.

Jesus clasps our trembling hand, and becomes our Fellow-traveller, leading us onwards with his own gentle hand through the Valley of the Shadow of Death, onward, ever onward, to our Eternal Home.

" Yea tho' I walk through the Valley of the Shadow of Death I will fear no evil, for Thou art with me ; Thy rod and Thy staff comfort me."

THE DEMON BIRD

AFTER Christmas, 1907, the Moor was covered with very deep snow for nearly a fortnight. On the virgin snow strange footprints were noted like those of a large bird, but its species could not be determined, and what was still more puzzling, they faced the wrong way. They had in previous years been noticed in time of snow. The superstitious folk said they were the tracks of the devil, who appearing in the form of a large bird, stalked about in the night.

During the great snows of 1916, 1917, 1927, 1929 these tracks were not seen. Has the devil left Dartmoor ? We hope so.

I base my lesson on this superstition, as there is so much in common between the devil's tracks and these footprints in the snow.

Like these footprints mar the virgin snow, so the devil mars the beautiful unsoiled lives of God's own children— he brands with his footprints.

Again, the demon bird is said to stalk under cover of darkness, so the devil moves much in the darkness, because his deeds are evil.

" Be sober, be vigilant ; because your adversary the devil, as a roaring lion, walketh about seeking whom he may devour."

BLACK GAME

ON the tongue of land which divides the Cut Water from the East Dart, one fine sunny afternoon in June, I came across a grey hen with her brood.

That faithful mother-bird taught a lesson. Black game are usually very wild, but this bird had her very young family with her to think about.

So she behaved just like a fussy hen with chicks, almost defiant, while her chicks disappeared one by one into the long heather ; when all had disappeared and were safe, she rose and flew away. Here is an instance of the care of the mother-bird.

We hear much of the Fatherhood and the Fatherliness of God, but we also hear of the great Mother Heart of God. "As one whom his mother comforteth, so will I comfort you, and ye shall be comforted in Jerusalem."

The Psalmist sings of the great Mother Heart of God : " He shall defend thee under His wings, and thou shalt be safe under His feathers."

And Our Lord proclaims the same truth : " O, Jerusalem, Jerusalem, thou that killest the prophets and stonest them that are sent unto thee, how often would I have gathered thy children together, even as a hen gathereth her chickens under her wings, and ye would not."

So in the dear kind God Who loves the world, you have a mother's heart, a mother's love, a mother's care, and a mother's breast, on which when you are lonely, sad, and sorrowful, and all seems so hopeless, you can rest your weary head and sob yourself to sleep in the sure hope of a bright to-morrow.

BOWERMAN'S NOSE

ALL who know the Moor around Manaton will have been struck with this curious freak—a solitary pillar of granite. It is of natural formation and consists of a core of granite, so hard that it has survived the ravages of time and storms. It is a good example of the weathering of the granite, the softer portions of the rock have worn away, the core remains, and is now so hard and durable, that it will probably last as long as the world lasts.

In a man the one thing that lasts is the soul, it even survives the catastrophe of death.

Much which goes to make up man as we know him, weathers and is worn away ; his eyesight, his physical strength, his powers of walking ; one thing survives is his soul.

It will survive the ravages of time and change, and even death. Man's animal body will perish, as the softer portions of Bowerman's Nose have weathered away the soul survives as an ensign on the top of a mountain, as a beacon on the top of a hill.

Bowerman's Nose is immovable, the soul of the man who dies in Christ is destined to become a pillar in the Temple of God in Heaven, and he shall go no more out.

GOLDEN BROOM

In the sunny month of June, as one crosses the Cherry Brook, on the road from Princetown to Postbridge, halt at the bridge and with your eye follow the river up the Valley, as it comes down from the Powder Mills.

The water is stained a deep chocolate brown by the peat ; fringing its banks and overhanging the stream is the glorious golden broom. Note the blending of the rich colours—the fresh bright yellow and gold of the broom, as it grows on the banks and overhangs the stream, with the rich deep brown of the peaty bank and the peat-stained water.

This is one of the most impressive blending of colours to be seen on the Moor.

Would to God our lives displayed a blending of colour so perfect as this. Now note this blending so pleasing to the eye could never be attained without light, and we see the colours heightened in the sunlight.

So the Light of Christ's Countenance and Presence must shine upon us and light up the colours and display the blending of the sweet graces of our life in Christ.

CLOUD SHADOWS

THERE is not a more entrancing scene on Dartmoor than the cloud shadows chasing each other o'er hill and dale on a stormy summer's day, when the lights and colours are good.

Each cloud casts its shadow, then passes on quickly to be followed by another.

Cloud *shadows* they are, yet how wonderfully they add to the glory of the landscape ; it is one of its chief glories.

Life has its storms, its sunshine and shadows. We sometimes complain when the shadow falls upon us, and for a moment life is rendered dark and gloomy ; but how soon it passes and all is sunshine again ; then another cloud, then out pops the sun again, and so on 'till life's little day is done.

I often think that when in the sunny glory of our Father's Home, we look back upon life, and think of the cloud shadows which have passed, often in quick succession across our life, that we shall see that the shadows were as necessary as the sunshine to make our life to be what our dear Father wants it to be.

THE CROSS SHOWS THE WAY

CONNECTING the Abbeys of Buckfast and Buckland, east to west, and Tavistock Abbey to Plympton Priory, north to south, are lines of crosses which mark the way across, what were in the ancient days, vast solitudes often without trodden paths.

Without something to guide them, travellers would be hopelessly lost. Dartmoor rivers are difficult to cross after rain, the fording places needed to be marked, direction was needed when the track forked, or when the pilgrim was in a valley and the distant scene was hidden from him.

These crosses are most ingeniously placed. Some mark the progress of the way across wide open parts of the Moor ; others, the fording places in the rivers ; others at a fork in the way, showing the direction to be taken, like our modern direction posts ; others on the sky-line on the hilltop to show the true direction to be taken ; others were so placed to warn the traveller to avoid danger spots— like bogs and swamps.

In life it is ever *the Cross* that shows the way, in darkness and perplexity, in fording the perils of rivers, in affording guidance when one comes to a fork in the road and one knows not which way to take, or in climbing the mountain of difficulty, or in avoiding on our journey the valleys of despondency with their swamps and shaky ground.

From your baptism to the hour of your death the Cross will always lead the way if you look for its guidance.

And as the hour of death approaches we lift our souls to our dear Lord and Saviour and pray :

> " Hold thou Thy Cross before my closing eyes ;
> Shine through the gloom and point me to the skies ;
> Heaven's morning breaks, and earth's vain shadows flee ;
> In life, in death, O Lord, abide with me."

CUT LANE

————

ALL the centre part of Dartmoor is one vast morass which runs for miles ; through the midst runs Cut Lane, the one safe passage from east to west, at all times ; all around bog always, fog and bog too often. Along this ancient way the moormen transfer their cattle from the eastern part of the Moor to the western, and conversely.

As we make our way through the world we find it full of perils and dangers on every side.

There is only *ONE WAY* through to safety—Christ THE WAY. If we follow CHRIST THE WAY, He will lead us safely through the mists and swamps and perils of life, and bring us to safety and rest.

> " Thou art the Way, the Truth, the Life.
> Grant us that way to know,
> That truth to keep, that life to win
> Whose joys eternal flow."

" IN THEIR DEATHS THEY WERE NOT DIVIDED "

WHEN the thaw came after the terrible blizzard of Christmas, 1927, the huge drifts melted very rapidly. As one melted near Cadover Bridge, out of it emerged three ponies all standing together—silent and still in death—frozen to death.

They had come together inspired by a common hope of surviving the storm, together they perished ; in their deaths they were not divided. When the storms of life overtake human beings, our social instincts draw us together—a common disaster evokes common sympathy ; yet no storm can destroy us, for we have with us One

" Whose Arm is mighty to save,"

watching us battling with the storm, ready to help and save us, if we will only stretch forth the hand of Faith—Jesus, who with a word stilled the storm on the lake of Galilee.

EPHRAIM'S PINCH

A MAN named Ephraim fell in love with the miller's daughter at Widecombe. The miller decided to test the strength of his prospective son-in-law. He told him that if he wished to marry his daughter he must carry a sack of corn from Widecombe to Postbridge without once putting it down. Ephraim in a rash moment accepted the wager. When he had covered $3\frac{1}{2}$ miles of the 5 miles, he reached the sharp bit of hill as he approached Runnage. Ephraim's heart did not prove strong enough for the occasion, and on this hill he collapsed with his sack, and died.

The moral is simple, don't do foolish things, and boast not thyself.

FLAXEN HAIR

NEAR Postbridge a friend of mine and the late Rev. S. Baring-Gould, were excavating a hut circle. Mr. Baring-Gould had left my friend a moment. During his absence my friend continued to dig, when he unearthed a bunch of flaxen hair.

Holding it up, and shouting with excitement, he said : " See what I have found—locks of hair of a fair Saxon girl."

In reply Mr. Baring-Gould said " It is the end of a cow's tail " ; and then he explained that someone in the neighbourhood had bewitched his neighbour's cows, and in consequence the cows were afflicted with all manner of disorders. To remove the spell, the man whose cows had been bewitched, had cut off the end of the tail of a cow belonging to the man who had bewitched them, and buried it there where no one was likely to find it.

This is one of the strange superstitions which survive on Dartmoor. Superstition dies hard. The way to remove it is to impart knowledge ; the truth will make them free— free from the bondage of superstition.

THE FOOTPRINTS OF THE MORNING

MANY years ago two friends went a day's journey on the Moor ; one knew the Moor, the other did not. An hour or so after starting, down swooped the fog and blotted out everything.

Both lost their way, and groped about for hours. Towards evening they found themselves in the bed of a stream, and noticed footprints on a bank of sand the previous winter's floods had washed up.

The one knew the ground at once, and realised they were at the head of the Erme—He said " These footprints are those we made this morning ; now I know where we are and how to steer our homeward course " ; soon they were out of their difficulties and homeward bound.

The footprints of the morning led them home.

Be careful where you plant your feet when you are young—follow with diligent care the footprints of the Son of Man. If the footprints of the morning of your life are clear and sharp, if you go astray in life, you will find your way back to the right path.

You will remember the kind mother who taught you the first rudiments of the Faith. She showed you how to make your first footprints.

If you have wandered off into a dreary fogbound land of neglect of religion, the remembrance of what mother taught you will make you feel you want to retrace your footsteps homewards. When you in your wanderings recover the road, remember this.

Along this road at Dawn of Day—the Day of the Christian Era—a Traveller passed, arrayed in glorious apparel, travelling in the greatness of His strength—One mighty to save—all along the road He has left His footprints, follow them patiently and they will bring you safely Home.

A SCENE OF UNIMAGINABLE GLORY

ON February 27th, 1928, Dartmoor was swept by an ice-storm of an intensity of which there is no known precedent. The whole Moor was covered by a sheet of ice ; hedges and trees covered with ice an inch thick in this part of the Moor, but 2½ inches in exposed places on the higher moors. This is called *Amel* (old English word which means enamel) and is caused by super-cooled rain or drizzle, which immediately freezes on the first object it touches, though at the moment the object it alights on may be above freezing.

When the sun came out here in the afternoon of February 27th, the country presented an amazing scene—every hedge and tree laden with ice and every blade of grass an icicle—and lit upon by the sunshine, displayed all the colours of the rainbow. In the strong wind the iced sticks clinked against each other like little bells, and ice crackled like paper. When the sun went behind a cloud much of the beauty was gone.

(See my Book on the " Great Ice-Storm," pub. Dec. 1929)

Lesson : Man is made in the image of God, and has in him much of the fair beauty of God built into him.

What he needs is illuminating with the Very light of the World ; then we see man as he is meant to be.

As the scene I have described was one of unimaginable glory when lit up by the sun, and so little without the sun; so is the life of a man illuminated by the Rays of the Light of the World. If Christ's light is withdrawn, all is so drab and dreary, the real beauty of man is not seen.

HAWK SWOOPING DOWN ON ITS PREY

OFTEN have I watched the hawk or the buzzard searching with his piercing eye the ground far beneath him, for his prey—a bird or a mouse, or a chick in a farmyard. Having found his prey, swoops down with one fell swoop, strikes it down and devours it.

> " Harpy-like not far away,
> The buzzard watches o'er his prey ;
> With piercing eye and rapid flight
> He skims the moor from morn 'till night.
> The feathered tribe are mute with dread
> At visage of his horny head ;
> And fiercely here he seems to reign,
> The pirate of the marshy plain."

Whenever I see the hawk swoop down on its prey, it impresses on me the lesson to be sharp in watching for our opportunities, and having found an opportunity swoop down upon it, as a hawk swoops down on its prey.

God provides our opportunities, and he bids us watch for them, and the moment we see them dart down on them like a hawk darts down on its prey, and seize and always use them to the best possible advantage.

A HIGH DAWN

A HIGH dawn is one that appears, not on the horizon, but above a bank of thick clouds, and so the first streak of dawn appears on the upper edge of these clouds, high up in the eastern sky—*a sure sign of rain*.

So in many a human life dense clouds of sin gather, banked one upon another, so that the dawn of day doth not appear in the life till high noon had been reached—*a sure sign of tears*. If all the morning of life's day has been clouded with sin, a long period of remorse and tears will follow.

Though the dawn broadens into day, and the sunshine of God's love lights up such a penitent life, the tears of remorse and sorrow will keep flowing 'till the soul has made its peace with God. Then when evening steals upon the life that has had a long rainy day, as the rain clouds roll away, the crimson glory of the setting sun bears promise of a bright to-morrow.

THE HONEY BEE

ONE of the pleasantest days one can spend on Dartmoor is a hot, summer's day, with the air perfumed with the sweet scents of the heather and the dwarf furze, with the ground carpeted with the rich blending of their purple and gold, the stillness of the air broken only with the hum of the busy bee as it flits from flower to flower to extract the delicious Dartmoor honey.

The honey bee is a worker and stores up honey for next winter.

" wiser than men."

All day long the honey bee works to add to its winter store for the colony to which it belongs.

God's will is that man should *work*—to get his own living and to store up against the future " if winter comes."

I heard recently of a young couple who married, both quite poor. When returning from the church to their home, the bridegroom said to his bride : " I have just enough left in my pocket to buy a drink with ; shall we go and spend it in the pub, or shall we go home and work ? " The bride answered : " If the decision rests with me, we will go home and work," and they did. Not many years after they had property worth £1,000. Sweet is the fruit of one's labour, so they found.

There is so much in our day to discourage thrift. Honest work has its sure reward. Learn from the honey bee the lesson to make provision for the future—for the possibilities of ill health, infirmity and old age.

AN ICE GROTTO

At Huntingdon Warren on March 5th, 1929, below the Clapper Bridge by which the cart-track crosses the Welsbrook, my eye was attracted by an ice-cased snow-drift, which projected from the bank of the stream, like a domed-shaped roof. Underneath was a most perfect ice-grotto, large icicles in clusters hanging from the roof to the stream, which was frozen over—a real gem in an ice-setting.

Of all the beautiful things I saw on that wondrous day, none were more beautiful than this.

Try to see and admire small things as well as large, both in the natural and the spiritual world.

The simple honesty in a cottage home is far more beautiful than the splendour in the house of princes. The cottage home built up from the sweat of the honest labourer's brow is sweeter than the palace of the wealthy. The simple humility and love of the holy and humble men of heart is more attractive than the power and state of the mighty.

A LARK WITH ITS MORNING SONG

ONE of the real delights on Dartmoor on a warm Spring morning is to hear the lark rise and soar higher and higher in the sky

" chanting its matins in the morning breeze "

with the air fragrant with the scents of the furze, and balmy with the warmth of returning day.

To the strong vigorous soul is there a higher joy than rising early and meeting our Lord in Sacrament at His Altar ? There is the Holiness of God's Presence.

" Holy, Holy, Holy, Lord God Almighty,
Early in the morning our song shall rise to Thee."

On Week-days you who have not the opportunity to come to Morning Prayer, to which the Matin bell calls us, let your first act of the day be the lifting up of your heart to God in prayer.

Christ has led the way : "Jesus rising up a great while before day retired into a solitary place and there prayed."

So our first act of the day should be the soaring heavenwards of our soul in prayer, like the lark rises high in the heavens with its morning song.

THE FIELD MOUSE

THERE is a dear little field mouse
" wiser than men "
which makes his hole facing south when a severe winter
is coming, but towards the north when we are in for a
mild wet open winter. This little mouse makes provision
for the future.

This is quite a little parable of life.

We have to make our home here, and how are we going
to place it--not towards the cold north facing the dreariness
and bleakness of the world, but towards the sunny south,
where your soul may bask in the bright sunshine of God's
Love, and there in His sunny Presence find protection
and warmth from the blasts of the world.

*It is appointed unto all men once to die, and after this
the Judgment.*

Death and Judgment we all have to face ; how are
you shaping your life and the lives of those dependent
on you to face these certain eventualities. Who are you
going to serve, Jesus Christ or the devil ? You are allowed
to make your *own* choice : which is it to be ?

Oh! that more had the wisdom of the little field mouse,
and make provision for the future, and instead of making
the soul face the world, would make it face God.

We should make our earthly home face one way—
heavenwards. We should *seek* Heaven—seek those things
which are above . . . *think* Heaven . . . set your affection
on things above, not on the earth.

THE ONE TAKEN AND THE OTHER LEFT

NEAR Owley Mill in a field, a fine ash tree was shattered by lightning in the evening of May 21st, 1928.

Under this tree were sheltering five cows, three were instantly killed, and two escaped injury. A day or two later I saw the surviving two grazing contentedly near by, as though nothing had happened, they appeared to have forgotten all about it. A man crossing the field at the time was unhurt, but the crash of the thunder was so terrific and prolonged, that he did not know what had happened.

The apparently arbitrary action of the lightning-flash teaches us a deep spiritual lesson : The separation of moral destiny. It is best explained by an example.

Two boys brought up in a Christian home, both have the same chances, the same parents' care, the same home comforts, the same tastes for amusements ; as far as one can see, there is no reason why both should not go straight.

On leaving home and starting out in life the separation comes.

The one sets out on an honourable career, and as years go on, develops a noble character and leads a most useful life.

The other goes hopelessly wrong, and speeds on his way to ruin and disgrace.

Christ came to those two young men as they were setting out in life, and gives to each the same call—" Follow Me."

The one responded, the other did not.
" The one was taken and the other left "

PATCHWORK PATTERN

I HAVE often seen in a Dartmoor farmhouse a piece of patchwork pattern, scraps of cloth, all colours of the rainbow and more besides, are stitched together to make a bright and attractive cover for a cushion, or a counterpane to keep people warm in bed during the bitter Dartmoor winter nights.

I often think that life is just like a patchwork pattern, some portions are bright and gay, some so dark and dreary ; some so interesting, some so drab.

But I am sure that when we see our life in the sunny light of our Father's Home, we shall see that the dark dreary colours of the patchwork of life—the pain, the sorrows, the disappointments, were just as needful as the bright and gay to make up God's perfect pattern of our life.

Of the dark dreary days of sorrow and pain and failure, as well as of the bright cheerful days of health and joy we shall say :

" He hath done all things well."

PEAT FIRES

————

"A lofty pile of well-dried peat
Imparts a strong and genial heat."

WHO is there who knows Dartmoor in winter has not felt the heat and seen the glow of the old peat fire. Until comparatively recent years peat was the only fuel used at the moorland farms, but times have changed. Some of these fires have never gone out for 100 years, for instance the Warren Inn.

In our spiritual life, what we need is a glowing zeal for the honour of God, and for the establishment of the standard of Righteousness taught by Chriist.

That glowing zeal, once kindled, should never be allowed to go out ; fanned by the gentle wind of the Spirit, it should be passed on from generation to generation, so that though men may come and men may go, the glow of the spiritual hearth of the home may be kept burning.

PURPLE AND GOLD

———

THE purple heather and the golden furze are the two glories of the rugged Dartmoor.

On the breezy slopes of Wind Tor near Widecombe-in-the-Moor, this glorious blending of purple and gold is seen to perfection on an August day.

Such perfect blending of colours in nature teaches us how beautiful our lives may become if we will only learn how to blend the Christian graces, which God has given to adorn the soul, and indeed for its equipment for action.

We must learn to blend firmness with kindness.

Firmness is an asset of real power in the life of a man, but if used alone, may become tyrannical.

If blended with true kindness how much is added to the power and usefulness of an active life.

So the perfect blending of purple and gold teaches us always to blend stern discipline with love.

Firmness with kindness
and strength with gentleness.

A RAY OF GLORY

DURING the very snowy winter of February-March, 1916, in the morning of March 9th, a tremendous fall of snow began soon after sunrise.

At 7-30, as I was watching the abnormally heavy snow, the thickly whitened country was instantly illuminated with a flash of lightning the most brilliant pink, instantly followed by a crash of thunder. The sight was so thrilling ; the brilliant pink on the snow for a moment of time, seemed like a ray of glory from the heavenly world ; but it was but a transitory flush—*the heavenly glory abideth.*

God speaks to our souls in these beautiful sights—does not the message of His Voice reach your ear ?

Often the sight is too thrilling for words—in the hush which falls upon us, God speaks.

RINGLESHUTTS

On debouching on the Moor above Holne after passing through Holne Gate, on the left in the distance are seen some old mine works. This is the old Ringleshutts mine abandoned long ago. There are considerable workings here, as the ground and the hillside beyond are scored with beams and pits.

Here long ago men came with a spirit of adventure, in bright hope of success, all seemed so promising, all so fair, the prospect seemed so bright.

Here the miners laboured, here they failed.

The lesson of Ringleshutts is the uncertainty of the success of human effort in material things.

On the other hand there is the absolute certainty of the triumphs of human effort in spiritual things eventually. Material effort fails, spiritual effort succeeds. Spiritual effort may sometimes appear to fail, but ultimate success is assured to those who wait for it and who co-operate with God.

We may not reap the fruits of our labour in this world, but they are in the safe-keeping of God, and in the next world God will bring them out of His treasure-house and present them to us.

ROSY GLORY

SUNDAY morning, February 17th, 1929, opened with a scene of surpassing beauty. The ground was covered with snow of immense depth ; trees, hedges, walls, buildings, were covered with a vast burden of snow. At sunrise the temperature was as low as 10 degrees F. Soon the whole snowscape was painted a lovely blush-rose colour toned down with a grey haze ; the trees and bushes looked as though that had been powdered with a powder-puff—it was a scene of unimaginable glory.

If the light of the sun which illuminates the world can produce scenes of such glory, what must the glory of the heavenly world be like, which is illuminated with the Effulgence of the Glory of God ? I often wonder.

A PAGAN SACRIFICE

———

ABOUT eighty years ago in a Dartmoor border parish, the cattle were afflicted with murrain and they were dying in numbers.

To appease the gods and secure the removal of the murrain, a farmer offered up a sheep in sacrifice to a pagan god—surely the high-water mark of superstition was reached on this occasion. Superstition is the devil's fraud.

When a visitation of God like this, comes and brings loss and trouble, trust God and pray for its removal.

Your trust will not be misplaced, your prayer will not be unheard.

CHEAP SALMON

For many years Mary Tavy had as its rector Rev. J. K. Anderson, a highly-cultured man and a polished gentleman. He took a leading part in the 'nineties in the field work of the Dartmoor Preservation Society, and was at all times a delightful companion. I called to see him one afternoon not very long before he died ; he was full of fun as usual.

He asked me if I liked salmon, and he added, " I get them for a shilling each." I said, " Let me into the secret."

His reply was : "A little way up the Tavy is a mine, the refuse from which renders the Tavy muddy.. The salmon get the sediment into their gills, and in their difficulties come up the small lateral stream which flows through my valley. They get stranded on the bank and die there. My parishioners say they are poisoned and won't eat them for fear of being poisoned themselves ; they bring them to me and I give them a shilling each for them, and often have an enjoyable dinner."

Ignorance deprived these villagers of fish diet which they might have enjoyed.

How much man loses through ignorance, and often, as in this case, persistence in ignorance.

Jesus invites : " Come learn of Me." If we would only respond, and go daily to Him, Who is the Universal Teacher and Universal Friend, how much we should gain in life, how many mistakes we should avoid, how much happier we should be.

SCOTCH BULLOCKS

ONE beautiful summer's day I was on the Moor, near Merrivale Bridge, when I came across a fine herd—about a dozen—of long horned Highland cattle, with their shaggy coats. I always admire these animals with their vari-coloured long, shaggy coats—red, black, brown, dun, grey, and white.

In the purple setting of the heather that summer's afternoon, they were especially beautiful, and made a lasting impression on my mind.

A few days later a terrible thunderstorm lasted all through the night—at Sheepstor we had a round twelve hours.

After that terrifying night eight of that noble herd were found in a newtake, all in a heap—killed by lightning.

As with these animals, looking so beautiful and fair one day and gone the next, so is the life of man.

Though he is endowed with an immortal soul, it is the tenant in this life of an animal body, subject to the same dangers and uncertainties as other animals.

As you and I are daily faced with such uncertainty of the tenure of life, let us prepare for the future. Live each day as if it were your last—*in Christ*.

" Be ye also ready, for in such an hour as ye think not the Son of Man cometh."

How often He comes suddenly.

A RED GLOW ON A SEA OF GLASS

" I saw a sea of glass mingled with fire." (Rev. xv., 2.)

As I passed the Water Oak Plantation above the Dean Valley, in the late afternoon of March 5th, 1929, there was a large snowfield on the east side of the plantation, covered with a sheet of ice, from the amel, which shone like a huge sheet of glass and reflected the trees on its mirror-like surface.

Through the dark pine trees came the blood-red rays of the setting sun, which gave this glassy sea a red glow.

In the Apocalyptic vision the Sea of Glass symbolises the course of Providence by which God conducts those who place themselves in His hands, to their final rest in His Presence.

The red glow on the Sea of Glass speaks of the fiery trials through which the saints and martyrs and the faithful had passed on their way to the Throne.

Life may have its fiery trials, but all forms a part of the wonderful working of God's Providence. Across the Glassy Sea, reddened with fire, is the way to the Throne of God and Home.

On that cold winter's afternoon, a sight so beautiful, a lesson so assuring, was to my soul a refreshing draught ; I drank long and deep, and then passed on refreshed and strengthened to cover the miles which lay between me and home.

As I watched the blood-red rays of the setting sun shining through the pine trees, casting a red glow on the glassy sea,

" I saw a sea of glass mingled with fire."

THE PLACE OF SHELTER

" William Stephens, Schoolmaster,
     Whose soul went into the place of shelter."

THIS is an epitaph on a tombstone in Morwenstow
Churchyard. A more appropriate epitaph could hardly
have been written on the tombstone of one who for years
lived in that storm-swept parish.

We all have to face the storms of life ; within the reach
of each of us is "*The* Place of Shelter "—God's Holy
Church. There the courts of the Lord are hallowed by
the Presence of A MAN, who is a hiding place from the
winds, a covert from the tempest and the shadow of a
Great Rock in a weary land. It is the dwelling-place of
God—God's House.

"Against this Holy Home
     Rude tempests harmless beat,
And Satan's angels fiercely come
     But to endure defeat."

Take your rest and shelter there 'till God gives the call
to leave it and your soul is carried by the angels into "*The*
Place of Shelter." There, under the Shadow of the Throne
the soul finds " the Place of Shelter " in the calm of
God's Presence.

AN ALTAR CLOTH OF SNOW

THERE is a delightful story told of an incident that happened at Lydford Church long years ago, one Sunday morning.

Through the night there had been a heavy drifting snow, and it had drifted in through a broken window and covered the altar with snow. The clerk said to the Vicar, " I will fetch a broom and sweep it off."

" No, no," said the Vicar, " leave it alone, God has spread His Table," and he celebrated the Holy Communion on Nature's altar-cloth of snow. How glad the joy of the Angels at seeing an Altar so fair, spread by the dear hand of God Himself.

Would not you like to have joined in that Holy Service, and met your God in Sacrament at the Altar covered with the snow of Heaven ? I should.

Yet in every village church, every Lord's Day, you may join in the Lord's Own Service, and meet your Lord in Sacrament at His Altar, spread with the fair linen cloth of the faultless Holiness of God, a covering far more beautiful and fair than the most spotless snow.

There He gives to us His dear Body and Blood, conveying to our weary souls the very life of the dear Lord Himself.

> The Service ended, onward we go,
> strengthened and refreshed,
> to face life's daily work.

THE SNOW CORNICE

OF all the wondrous architectural works of the snow, *the cornice* is one of the most beautiful.

I will explain how it is formed.

First the level on the windward side of a wall or hedge is reached by the drifting snow. *Then*, on the other side of the wall, the ledge begins to form, slightly curved in section, the ledge being undercut like a volute in sculpture. On the sheltered side below there is a kind of gentle undercurrent of air, the action of which keeps the accumulation of snow a foot or two away from the wall, according to its height ; but also to blow the drifting particles up against the under side of the growing ledge, which is then thickened both *from above* and *below*, as well as helped to grow in the direction of its extension.

Thus is formed the snow cornice, one of the most beautiful things in nature.

There are several contributory causes which make a life beautiful, without which the life will neither grow nor develop strength—purity of life, honesty of purpose, a kindly disposition, a sweet reasonableness, and definite goodness and real spiritual power.

The wind needed to weld these together and make a beautiful life, is the gentle breeze of the Spirit of Grace

> " 'Tis His that gentle voice we hear,
>   Soft as the breath at even,
> That checks each fault, that calms each fear
>   And speaks of Heaven."

A SNOW DAM

DURING the great snowstorm of Christmas night, 1927 (see my book *The Great Blizzard of Christmas*, 1927, pp. 17, 18), a huge drift formed right across the Shavercombe Valley, and the water brought down by the stream, from the heights above, had formed a small reservoir. On the night of the thaw, when the mighty rush of the waters of the torrential rain and the melting snows came down, the dam burst and carried all before it.

Note the dam which impounded the waters was artificial. So great danger is often incurred by preventing freedom of speech. Hyde Park orators let off superfluous steam, and it acts as the safety-valve of an engine saves the boiler from bursting. So if freedom of speech is not allowed, but pent up, the burst will come sooner or later, just as the unnaturally impounded waters burst the snow dam in the Shavercombe Valley.

A GREAT DRIFTING SNOW

A SIMPLE lesson of great power may be learnt by us all from the cause of a great drifting snow which often buries the Dartmoor walls and fill its lanes.

It is concentration of power.

These are the causes of the snowdrifts:

(1) A large quantity of snow.
(2) Gale of wind.
(3) Frost.
(4) Something to arrest the blowing snow, like a hedge, a wall, or a gate.

Now if even one of these conditions is lacking, the snow will not drift; each condition is absolutely necessary, and it is only by a concentration of all these conditions that the wonderful accumulations of snow are formed.

We need seriously to learn the need of concentrating all our powers; our knowledge, our strength, our skill, our opportunities, our industry, and our hands uplifted in prayer.

Every scrap of power we can bring to bear upon a given task must be brought into service, and concentrated on the one work in hand. Then through the help of our God we shall succeed.

SNOW FOUNTAIN

THIS is an interesting phenomenon in a Dartmoor snow-storm.

These are the conditions necessary : a drifting snow, a wall piled up with snow on the windward side within a foot of the top. A strong wind of fluctuating strength.

As the icy blast drives the snow, it strikes the wall and rises and falls like a fountain, several feet high, as the wind increases or decreases in strength.

Our Lord instructs us that the wind is a figure of the Divine Spirit. The more the Spirit of God blows on the soul of a man with His life-giving breath, so the soul rises heavenwards. If withheld, the soul sinks.

St. Paul told the Colossians we are to *seek* heaven and *think* heaven. The power which wafts our minds and hearts heavenwards is the wind of the Divine Spirit, as He blows the fountain of our life rises, if He ceases it subsides.

> So as the snow-fountain depends on the strength of the wind for its rise and fall, so our soul depends on the strength with which the Spirit blows upon us to strengthen, guide and illuminate us.
> " Come Holy Ghost thy people bless."

A SNOW TUNNEL

AFTER the amazingly rapid thaw on the night of January 1st, 1928, after the Great Blizzard, when nearly three inches of rain fell in the night, causing great floods, I several times saw one curious effect. †

Great snowdrifts blocked the watercourses, and the water being dammed up, got away by boring a tunnel under the snow, the drift remained with a clear-cut tunnel under it.

So you cannot stay the onward course of truth—which is like a flowing stream ; you may block the ordinary channel through which it pursues its course, but it will percolate through somehow, and will not be stayed.

Truth cannot be hidden or stayed indefinitely.

How many illustrations of this occur in every generation in the onward course of Christian truth. Why ? Because Christ the Truth is invested with infinite power, infinite knowledge, and He is daily giving light to an ignorant world, and overcoming every obstacle to the onward flow of truth throughout the world.

† See " The Great Blizzard of Christmas, 1927," p. 11.

VIRGIN SNOW

———

I ALWAYS think that the virgin snow is the most beautiful thing in the natural world.

Nowhere is it better seen than on the wilds of Dartmoor, where you may see miles without a track or stain of any kind. It is to me the symbol of a stainless world untrodden by the foot of sinful man.

It is the wickedness of man which stains and sullies the beautiful world we live in.

I always take pleasure in tramping across the wastes of virgin snow, for it is pleasant to find sometimes an environment without track and without stain of any kind.

The stainless whiteness of such a land brings to our mind the stainless whiteness of the heavenly world. White is the colour of Heaven, but the heavenly white is not the dull white of snow, but the glittering white of heaven, the white which catches and reflects with dazzling effect the light of the Divine Glory and Presence.

Before the Great White Throne we shall stand.
The White Stone will be given to the victor.
The faithful will be clad in White Raiment.

Those who have come through the great tribulation of earth will be arrayed in the White Robes of the Heavenly Glory.

STEPPING-STONES LEADING TO THE
GATE OF HEAVEN

As we approach Meavy from Lynch Hill, at the foot of which, under the spreading oak is Marchant's Cross—which pointed to the fording place to cross the river below. Here travellers of days of long ago knelt and prayed for Heavenly light and protection to guide them on the journey across the lonely bleak Moors.

The cross shows the way to the fording-place across the river, now marked by stepping-stones. In olden days there was no bridge, and the stepping-stones then led across the stream to the Gate of Heaven—Meavy Church.

As we journey on in life, we must search out stepping-stones, which will bridge the stream of time and lead us to the Gate of Heaven. The Cross will guide you to find the stepping-stones.

A RED SUNRISE

On February 13th, 1929, during the great frost, the snow lay deep upon the ground and all was wrapped with Nature's white quilt.

Presently the sky became brilliantly crimson, the heavens seemed in flames. The surface of the snow caught this blaze of glory and reflected it, the snow went a rich pink.

After a few minutes it all faded away and left the steel grey of a winter's day.

It was but a transitory flush of glory ; what a contrast with the abiding glory which will illuminate and render beautiful our lives in Eternal Day ; our lives even here catch and reflect the first rosy glow of the Dawn of the Eternal Morning.

> " The roseate hues of early dawn,
>   The brightness of the day,
> The crimson of the sunset sky,
>   How fast they fade away.
> Oh, for the pearly gates of Heaven,
>   Oh for the golden floor,
> Oh, for the Sun of Righteousness
>   Which setteth never more."

SWEET SCENTS

WHO has lived on Dartmoor who does not know the sweet scents of the Moor—that of the furze bloom on a warm Spring day, or of the purple heather in August, or in the cool freshness at the close of a hot summer's day the delicious scent of the venn, which rises from the peat soil which has been baked with the sun all day, and gladdens the heart of man.

There is a sweet smell which gladdens the Heart of God—the offering to God of our best.

After Noah came out of the Ark, the first thing he did was to build an altar and offer to God a sacrifice. "And the Lord smelled a sweet savour "—that is to say, it gave God pleasure to see such an offering, and He accepted it gladly.

Christ's offering His life to God was to God a sweet-smelling savour, the offering to God of His life without blemish and without stain was gladly accepted by the Eternal Father.

May you, when you smell again the sweet scents of the Moor, whether of the golden furze or of the purple heather, or of the venn, remember that when you make your offering to God, do so with this resolution—I am making my offering to God, therefore I will give Him the best that I can.

THE WINDSTREW

AT the back of the ruins of the old Longstone Manor House, the old home of the Elfords, at Sheepstor, in the middle of a field is a granite platform ; this is the thresh-floor or windstrew where the Elfords of Longstone threshed their corn. I remember it more than twenty years ago with granite steps, and on one of the steps was carved, "J.E. 1640 (John Elford) ; a similar inscription occurs in the hour-glass above the porch of Sheepstor Church.

This is much like the threshing-floor of the Bible ; in Palestine these granite platforms are cut out of the rock on the hillsides, where like the Longstone windstrew, they can catch all winds.

Its spiritual message is that of the coming Judgment.

Two events lie before us, Death and Judgment.

Each of us will stand before the judgment-seat of Christ, *each* will give an account of himself to God, *each* faithful servant will receive the rewards of his labours, *each* of the faithful will have the unspeakable joy of the vision of God's Face.

Let us lay very deeply to heart these words of John the Baptist, speaking of Christ :

" Whose winnowing fan is in His hand, and He will thoroughly purge His threshing floor, and gather His wheat into the garner ; but He will burn up the chaff with unquenchable fire."

INDEX.

	Page
Ammil	18
Beardown Man	6
Bee, the Honey	21
Bird, the Demon	7
Bullocks, Scotch	34
Bowerman's Nose	9
Broom, Golden	10
Cloud Shadows	11
Cross shows the way, The	12
Cut Lane	13
Dawn, a high	20
Death, not divided, In	14
Ephraim's Pinch	15
Flaxen Hair	16
Footprints of the Morning	17
Game, Black	8
Glory, a ray of	29
Glory, Rosy	31
Glory, a scene of Unimaginable	18
Hawk and its prey	19
Heather, White	5
Ice Grotto	22
Lark with its Morning Song	23
Mouse, the Field	24
Patchwork Pattern	26
Peat Fires	27
Preface	3
Purple and Gold	28
Ringleshutts	30
Sacrifice, a Pagan	32
Salmon, cheap	33
Scents, Sweet	46
Sea of Glass	35
Shelter, place of	36
Snow, an Altar Cloth of	37
Snow Cornice	38
Snow Dam	39
Snow, Drifting	40
Snow Fountain	41
Snow Tunnel	42
Snow, Virgin	43
Stepping Stones	44
Sunrise, a Red	45
Taken, One	25
Windstrew, The	47

A NEW DARTMOOR SERIES.

THE DARTMOOR FOREST SERIES.

No. 1.   Ready 1930.   **Dartmoor Forest**—South.

No. 2.   Ready 1931.   **Dartmoor Forest**—West.

No. 3.

No. 4.   **The Heart of Dartmoor.**   Price 1/6.   Post 2d.
         (North-East and Centre).

No. 5.   **A Dartmoor Snowstorm**   Price 1/6.   Post 2d.
         (The Great Blizzard of Christmas, 1927).

No. 6.   **A Great Winter on Dartmoor** (1928–29)—with
         accounts of the unprecedented snowstorm at Dean
         Prior of February 16th, 1929, and the Great Ice Storm
         of the closing days of February.
                    Ready Christmas, 1929.   Price 1/-   Post 1½d.

A NEW SERIES.

THE WORD PICTURES OF THE BIBLE.
                              In Parts, 1/- each.   Post 1½d.
Being a Collection of the Metaphors and Similies of the
Bible with their Lessons.

New Testament, *Part 1.   "Some Aspects of Life."
                    Now Ready.   Price 1/-   Post 1½d.

   Part 2.   "Some Picturesque Scenes in the New Testament."
                              Ready Lent, 1930.

   Part 3.   "Some Lessons from Bird and Animal Life in the
             New Testament."   Ready Advent, 1930.

A NEW SERIES.

THE SPIRITUAL LESSONS FROM NATURE SERIES.

No. 1.   *Spiritual Lessons from Dartmoor Forest.**
         Part 1.   "White Heather" and other Studies.
                    Now Ready.   Price 1/-   Post 1½d.
         Part 2.   "Crystal Streams" and other studies.
                    Ready 1930.   Price 1/-   Post 1½d.

---

* *These two new books have a very limited edition, therefore will
those who want them please order them without delay.*

Part 11

"Crystal Streams"

and other studies

Spiritual Lessons
from
Dartmoor Forest

PART 2.
"Crystal Streams" and other studies.

By the Rev. H. HUGH BRETON, M.A.

Author of "Beautiful Dartmoor," "The Breezy Cornish Moors," "Land's End and
The Lizard," "The North Coast of Cornwall," "Morwenstow," "Hawker of
Morwenstow," "The Heart of Dartmoor," "The Word Pictures of the Bible," &c
[see cover back

" In the shade, but shining;
Reflecting the Light, that shineth
more and more unto the Perfect Day."

Spiritual Lessons
from
Dartmoor Forest

PART 2
" CRYSTAL STREAMS "
and other studies.

By
The Rev. H. HUGH BRETON, M.A.

Author of 'Beautiful Dartmoor,' 'The Breezy Cornish
Moors,' 'Lands End and The Lizard,' 'The North
Coast of Cornwall,' 'Morwenstow,' 'Hawker of
Morwenstow,' 'The Heart of Dartmoor,' 'The Word
Pictures of The Bible.' &c.

Price 1/-   Postage 1½d.

PRINTED & PUBLISHED BY
RIDOUTS LIMITED.
WHITSTABLE, KENT,
1930.

PREFACE.

THESE little meditations are rough-shaped like the granite boulders which strew the slopes of the Dartmoor mountains. I hope they may appeal to lovers of Dartmoor and be a little help and refreshment to them, to soul as well as body.

Nature has many spiritual lessons to teach those who have the spiritual eye to see and the spiritual mind to learn.

The illustrations are not drawn from the imagination, but from actual observations of nature, which is ever ready to convey spiritual lessons to a spiritual man.

If this little volume is acceptable and helpful to my readers, several other parts will follow. It has bright little companions—" The Word Pictures of the New Testament," Part I., " Some Aspects of Life," and Part II. " Personal Religion," now ready.

H. HUGH BRETON.

DEAN PRIOR VICARAGE, BUCKFASTLEIGH.
  March 1st, 1930.

NOTE.—The Books may be purchased from the Author.

CRYSTAL STREAMS.

" As the hart panteth for the waterbrooks so panteth my
soul for Thee O God."

ONE of the most delightful features of the Dartmoor
country is its streams; nowhere but in a granite
country could streams be so crystal clear.

Much is added to their beauty by the rugged
country through which they pursue their course—
through deep valleys crowned by giant tors with their
weather-worn rocks. The crystal stream flows through
this wild lovely country, fed by lateral streams,
gathering volume as it goes.

The Dartmoor tourist can learn many lessons of
great spiritual value from these mountain streams.

Jesus spoke of Living Water, meaning water running
ceaselessly from a spring, and by Living Water He
meant *His own life*.

I. The crystal stream has *its source* in a vigorous
spring.

The source of the Exe on Exmoor is a fine example
of this—from a raised quagmire the Exe rises and
gushes for a powerful stream at its beginning.

A Living Stream as crystal clear
Welling from out the Throne
Of God and of the Lamb on high
The Lord to man hath shown.

II. The living stream has *its beauty*—the clear,
sparkling, splashing water speaks of the beauty of the
pure life of Jesus seen during His life on earth, and
reflected in the beautiful lives of His saints through
the centuries since.

III. *Again,* there is *its life-giving power*.

" Everything shall live whither the river cometh."

Where streams of Living Water flow there is life
abundant.

THE CRYSTAL STREAM IN ACTION.

As the stream flows on *it gathers in volume* as it proceeds on its course.

How true this is of the Life of Jesus.   Think for a moment of the vast tracts of the world where His Life was unknown 200 years ago and well known to-day and gives life to millions.

" Everything liveth whither the Living Water flows."

There is not only its beauty but there is also *its power to work*.

In its onward course water is often diverted from a river and conveyed by a leat or mill-stream to turn mills or work machinery.

What may not be accomplished if the Life of Jesus —the Living Water—is brought into our individual life, or into our home, or into our parish.

In all these different spheres it is the Living Water, the Life of Jesus, which will work such wonders.

The channels through which it is brought to us are the Means of Grace He has Himself appointed.   See pages 10, 25.

He invites you to come and use them

Listen to His Loving Invitation :

" Let him that is athirst come.
    And whosoever will, let him take the water of life freely."

THE THREE BOYS.

AT the south end of Shovel Down, 2 miles S.W. of Kestor, are the ruins of a small Cromlech, known as The Three Boys, which was destroyed a long time ago. Still standing erect is one of the supporting stones of the Capstone, which is lying on the ground a few yards to the southward. Some of the stones have been taken to build the newtake wall hard by.

This was once a stately monument tho' small, and the grave of some prehistoric worthy.

The great principle which should inspire the life of every Christian is to build up and edify, not to destroy.

Man, through the devil in him, too often leaves everywhere the print of the cloven hoof of destruction.

Always set before you the Prince of Life who came not to destroy but to build up. Never destroy anything that is good, but go steadily on, building as you go, adding stones and strength to the City of God.

CALA RAG WHETLOW.

"A straw for a talebearer."

THIS is the Cornish motto on the Arms of the Carminow Family to be seen in Talland Church, near Looe.

On a very calm day the slight movement of a straw on the thatch of a stack tells which way the wind is blowing.

It is the little things that tell.

Cala rag whetlow.

A look will convey to you the attitude of a man's mind, whether he is friendly or hostile.

The tone of his voice what he wishes his words to convey.

Even the modulation of his voice will show you whether he means to emphasise a statement or not.

A hasty word spoken in an outburst of anger will often manifest more truly the real attitude of a person's mind towards you than all his conversation at other times.

A single act of underhandedness will tell you a man's character.

A profane word will tell you what manner of man he is.

"A man's gait and excessive laughter show what he is."

Cala rag whetlow.

If one sees a well-dressed, neatly-groomed man, let him open his mouth and speak you will quickly know what his education is.   So in spiritual things.   Note how a man values his Communion, how he comports himself in Divine Service, his interest in the Scriptures, and you will discern his Spiritual nature.

Cala rag whetlow.

CHICKEN SCRATCHING ABOUT FOR A LIVING.

―――――――

" My mate is like a chicken that has to do a lot of
scratching for a living."

THIS witty observation was made to me by one of
the men building Dean Vicarage wall to-day—Aug.
15th, 1929.

It is a common sight on a Dartmoor farm, as
elsewhere, to see fowls diligently scratching in the
dust for insects, or around a corn stack for grains of
corn, in this way they do their bit to toil for a living.

A law common to the natural and to the spiritual
world is that man should work for his living. In
everyday life the idler comes to want.

In the spiritual world the man who does not strive
after spiritual things becomes weak by the operation
of the law of degeneration.

Many seek but do not find, because they have not
perseverance to scratch deep enough.

The man who finds the grains of heavenly gold and
becomes rich with spiritual wealth is the man, who
daily approaches the Throne of Grace in his private
prayers, who Sunday by Sunday attends the Sanctuary
of God and joins in the worship and praise of God.
Or the man who regularly comes to his early
Communion, or the one who walks miles through
country lanes to his Communion on the Lord's Day.
These are the laws of God, and the law of Thy mouth
is dearer unto me than thousands of gold and silver.

CONVERGING PATHS.

On Butterdon Hill several well-defined paths converge from N. S. E. and W.—sheep tracks. They radiate from one point—a large pool of fresh water where animals resort to quench their thirst—sheep and cattle, foxes and badgers, ponies young and old.

There is one pool to which we must all find our way if we are to live—the Spring of Everlasting Life—Jesus Christ.

Animals cannot live without water, hence they wear these beaten tracks to their drinking places.

The Spring of Everlasting Life is reached by converging paths.

(a) One of these is *Prayer*; this is a sure way of access and as years roll on the path should become well worn with use.

Prayer is not an inactive state of the soul, but it is movement—the movement of the soul towards God.

The spiritual man who prays feels want, and his soul moves towards the means of supply of his need—JESUS.

(b) Another path of approach—*the Holy Scriptures* —here is a well of life—a medium through which God pours his life-giving Spirit into our lives.

(c) The golden path of approach is *the Blessed Sacrament*; in this the King of Glory, crowned with many crowns, comes and invites us to feed on Him and drink of His Precious Blood; here He gives to us His own Life, His own Strength, His own Saving Grace.

CROSSES ALONG THE WAY.

How often the way across the desert of the Moor is marked by Crosses, some mark a fording place in a river, some point the way like modern direction posts.

As we journey along the road of life Crosses mark the way.

The Cross takes different forms, sometimes a poignant sorrow, or an irreparable loss, or some keen disappointment; each, as we pass them if viewed in the right way and manfully borne, will be a definite help to us on our journey to Heaven.

Each cross thus borne marks a new advance, an accession of fresh strength, a brighter outlook, renewed hope for the next onward stage.

Each cross is God's appointment, each is placed at *the right place* on our road.

" Take up thy Cross the Saviour said."

Among the Oxyrynchus Papyri letters dug out of the sands of Egypt this pathetic prayer has been found : —

" O God of the crosses that are laid upon us, help thy servant."

God is regarded at once as the sender and the mitigator of trials.

When our Lord appoints our crosses on our journey, may He place His dear shoulder under them and help us bear them and mitigate the trials they impose upon us.

CURIOSITY.

ONE very dark night after preaching at Shaugh I was walking home, and as soon as I got out on the open moor a fox began to bark, it followed me on my right hand at a distance of about 100 yards to Cadover Bridge, where it crossed the Plym and went through Brisworthy Plantation, and it did not leave me till I reached Ringmoor Cot.

This was nothing but curiosity.

One often sees the same thing in human beings, but it is not good to satisfy the curiosity of a prying mind.

Never intrude yourself into affairs of others—in other words always mind your own business.

Most quarrels arise, many friendships are broken up, a vast amount of mischief arises through people not minding their own business.

A well-known Frenchman was once asked what he considered to be the leading trait in the character of Englishmen. The answer instantly came—intruding themselves into things which do not in the least concern them.

We should suppress a prying curiosity. Christ was once asked to interfere in a dispute and the answer came : " Man who made me a judge and a ruler over you." He declined to interfere.

So suppress your curiosity and don't interfere in the affairs of others.

A DESERTED ROAD.

RUNNING parallel to the Main Road here at Dean is a deserted road, which, as it approaches the Village at Higher Dean, runs through a deep cutting through the rocks. This is the old coach road from Plymouth to London.

Time was when this rocky gully resounded with the old post horn, announcing to Dean the approach of the London Coach, and with the clatter of the horses' hoofs, and the rattling and creaking of the Stage Coach.

All is deserted and silent now, and all that remains is the road grown over with grass, brambles and thorns.

I often think this deserted and forgotten road is a warning to us what becomes of our life, if we neglect it and allow it to become derelict. Soon the rank weeds of bad habits cover our path, then as a result of long neglect briars and thorns of evil overgrow it.

This is a picture of the degeneration and desolation of the soul when it ceases to be the Way of the Spirit of God.

BETWEEN THREE FIRES.

I WATCHED with interest on March 1st, 1929, a pair of herons hovering over Reddicleave Brakes. Dartmoor was covered with a sheet of ice through the ammil; a piercing East wind moaned across the icy plain, trees, bushes and furze glittered with the ammil in the morning sun.

The herons were famished with hunger and their fleshless breasts looked like knives as they turned in the sunlight.

Wheeling around them was a hungry buzzard striving to get above them and strike a mortal blow. As they hovered, in their cries they seemed to say-- we are between three fires.   If we go inland in search of food we face the farmer's gun; if we stay here we are in danger of being cut down by this moor eagle watching us with piercing eye; if we go out into the moor with its frozen streams and ice covered ground, we risk being frozen to death.

After much hesitation their mind was made up, and they acted promptly and flew off towards the Moor— they decided to face starvation on the Moor with a possibility of surviving, than being shot by the farmer's gun, or being killed in cold blood and devoured by the Moor eagle.

No doubt their decision was right for in a few days the hot sun thawed the streams and the ice on the Moor.

When you find yourself beset by difficulties like this, give serious thought and seek Divine Guidance how to act and make a decision.   When you have made your decision act swiftly with determination.

FOREST FIRES.

So many of these are caused by mischievous people setting fire to the forest.

Implanted in man's nature is the love of destruction and it finds full play on Dartmoor, where fires are so common.

In the Spiritual world there is a fire of iniquity which does immense harm once it is started—the tongue and the mischievous words it drops. (See Word Pictures of the Bible, Part 2, on *" The Forest Fire."*).

But there is quite another aspect to the part the activities of the tongue work. It may play a nobler part, it may set on fire with a heavenly fire (Acts II. 3. Isaiah VI. 6. Jeremiah V. 14).

Philo illustrates the growth of goodness in the soul.

" As the smallest spark will, if duly fanned, kindle a vast pyre, so is the least aliment of virtue capable of growth until the whole nature of man glows with a new warmth and brightness."

The Tongue, while capable of great mischief, is also capable of doing immense good. One utterance of a man of God will convert souls, and bring them into the way of everlasting salvation.

One word of a Statesman will bring peace and happiness to a whole continent.

Let your tongue each day drop a spark of the Divine Fire, which will kindle in the hearts of your fellow men a zeal for God, for God's Life, for God's Laws and God's people; a fire which shall spread with the rapidity of the forest fire, not to hurt but to help, not to destroy but to purify, not to char and blacken, but to illuminate with a light which shines from the lives of God's good men, " whose path is as the shining light that shineth more and more unto the Perfect Day."

GINGAFORD.

WHEN you build a house you must have water, water supply often settles the site of a house.

Many a Dartmoor Cot is built close to a stream, and when there is no stream the water supply has to be conducted to the house by a leat.

To the N.W. of Brent Hill, below Gingaford Cross, is the small ruined farm named Gingaford, situated in a depression in the fields. Through this depression and past the house flows a streamlet, which gushes out of the wall opposite the farm-house door to supply the old house.

As man's body needs water, so his soul needs the living water—the Spirit of Jesus, to sustain his soul.

Some are fortunately placed, because as soon as they understand the world they are born into, they find their life placed, like a Dartmoor Cot with a streamlet flowing by, beside the Living Water. The home has been built up by Christian parents and has the Life of Christ flowing by and into the home, quietly refreshing every sphere of their life.

With others the Living Water had to be brought to the home, like water that is brought to a cot by a leat.

It may be a visit from their parish clergyman or a friend has brought water from the Wells of Salvation —the agents through whom Christ conducts the living water to the soul.

Jesus said :—" Whosoever drinketh of the water that I shall give him shall never thirst, but the water that I shall give him shall be in him a well of water springing up into everlasting life."

A CHIEFTAIN'S GRAVE.

ON Yellowmead Down, Sheepstor, is a stone monument of distinction—a miniature Stonehenge.

It consists of four concentric circles, formerly running away from it in a S.W. direction were several parallel stone rows of which fragments only now remain.

These circles formerly enclosed the grave of some Moorland Chief, whose clansmen honoured by erecting this elaborate monument.

My last work for the parish of Sheepstor in 1921 was to erect the fallen and buried stones of this monument —116 in all. The monument teaches us the lesson to honour the dead. Prehistoric man held his dead in high honour. We Christian people should not forget our dead, but have them in everlasting remembrance, because we know that they are still alive —they have passed on to the higher life.

> " For Christ our Lord was buried once,
> He died and rose again,
> He conquer'd death, He left the grave;
> And so will Christian men."

A GOLDEN SUNSET.

On the day of the Great Ammil, Feb. 27, 1929, as the
sun was sinking in the Golden West, the ice which
covered hedges, trees, fields, etc., was turned into a
rich golden colour from the sun's rays which seemed to
cover the scene with a flood of gold. The landscape
was glittering, sparkling, scintilating, flashing divers
colours, as tho' Nature was preparing to spend the long
hours of the night holding High Festival with the scene
illuminated with coloured lights.   Near at hand and
in the far distance on the sky line the bushes on the
tops of the hedges glittered and shone like electric
torches.

If the setting sun can illuminate the icescape and
create such indescribable glory, what will the glory of
the Eternal Morning be, when the Rising Sun appears
above the horizon of the world with healing in His
Wings?

Don't you often wonder?   I do.

AN ICY SPRING.

ON Hillsboro' Hill, near Sheepstor, after passing the mine buildings, on the left side of the cart track is a wonderful spring which gushes forth from the bowels of the earth, and then crosses the track and flows down into Evil Combe. Its water is as cold as ice, as it wells up from a great depth. Only those who have drank of the pure crystal clear water of such an icy spring know how refreshing and invigorating it is on a hot day.

(At this spring the peat cutters fill their large jars on their way out to the Peat Tyes near Broad Rock).

Yet this is a feeble image of the refreshment that comes to the soul that drinks of Christ the Living Water.

As any hard worker goes on year after year he begins to feel the burden and heat of the day, but when he feels faint and weary, at hand is the Spring of Everlasting Life in which he can drink and find strength and refreshment.

I heard the Voice of Jesus say,

" Behold, I freely give
The living water, thirsty one
Stoop down, and drink, and live:"
I came to Jesus, and I drank
Of that life-giving stream;
My thirst was quenched, my soul revived,
And now I live in Him.

A LONELY GRAVE.

HIGH up in the valley of the Avon, just before in its southward course from the bogs it forms an elbow and flows eastward, is an old pack horse bridge which spans the river.

Standing above this about 100 yards due south is an interesting sepulchral monument of a prehistoric chief. (See " Dartmoor Forest," Part III.   Avon Valley.)

It is a double circle of standing stones within which the interment has taken place. No doubt the dead chief, in whose honour this monument was raised, had lived in the prehistoric village on the opposite side of the Valley.

Between the living and the dead flowed the river Avon.

Here is a little parable.

The living in this world are divided from the dead (those who have gone before) by the narrow stream of death.   Divided now, the day is coming when the narrow stream of death will be swallowed up and be no more, and the living and the dead will be one, gathered together into One Flock under One Shepherd —the Good Shepherd Who gave His Life for the Sheep, and hath swallowed up death in victory.

MISTS.

STANDING on the top of Yennadon Down, one may see a veil of mist filling Meavy Valley; go down into the Valley and you will scarcely perceive its existence.

Sin is a mist just like this, it is so deceptive that the sinner hardly realises its existence, but there it is—a very real blighting, deadening vapour about us, around us, within us.

The way to realise it is to ascend the hill of moral eminence and look down upon it.

It is when a man abandons a life of sin, and receives from Jesus Himself the forgiveness of sins and the cleansing of the soul from its stains, and then with his purified and strengthened life ascends to a higher level in the Spiritual world, that he comes to realise the reality of sin.

" Lead me to the Rock that is higher than I." .

It was from an exceeding high mountain that the sinless Jesus saw all the Kingdoms of the world and the glory of them, and apprised the world and its glory at their true values.

So when Christ has purified our life and we ascend, led by His gentle Hand, to a higher plane, we see the true character of sin, and the world, and its vanities.

LUMINOUS MOSS.

THIS often is seen in the crannies of walls facing north and in caves and caches.

It is due to phosphoresence.

It needs *the light* and *the shadow* to show up its beauty.

So we need sorrow to know the Divine Compassion; we need difficulties to teach us the Divine Aid.

Without our weaknesses should we ever feel God's strength.

If life had no dangers, should we learn to lean on the Protecting Power of God?

If we, in our earthly pilgrimage, need *the shadow,* we also need *the light.*

Take the luminous moss from its cranny, and it looks nothing but a handful of earth; in its cranny the shadow and the light make it illuminate the place where it grows.

Some men can never be their own master, they ever need the discipline and guidance of authority. Without these they are useless, with them they shine.

Again there is many a life made strong and useful through both shadow and sunshine. There falls across the life the shadow of God's chastening Hand. and there is the sunshine of God's Love and Fresence, which illuminate, warm, cheer and stir into action the activities of the life.

MOSS ON BOULDERS.

FEW things we see on the Moor that delight the lover of Nature more than the vari-coloured mosses which grow on the granite boulders in the rivers and on the hillsides; red, black, green, grey, yellow, brown, chestnut, in fact most colours are to be found; it is strange it grows so well on the stone.

But notice :

(1) This moss will not grow *without moisture,* and therefore needs a moist climate.

What may not grow on your stony heart if only the dews of Heaven fall copiously upon it.

One kind of growth can thrive there—the fair graces with which God adorns the Christian soul—love, joy, peace, goodness, etc.

But without the moisture of the dew of God's Grace they won't grow.

(2) The growth of mosses on the boulder is very slow. And slow is the growth of the graces of the Christian soul. We have need of patience for tho' their growth is slow, it is sure and imperishable, for they spring up into everlasting life and adorn the soul in the next world.

NOAH IN HIS ARK.

AT Huntingdon Warren after the Great Snowstorm of February 16th, 1929, Mr. and Mrs. Waye were shut in their Warren House as completely as Noah was shut in the Ark at the Flood, not with water, but with snow. There they had to stay nearly three weeks.

Their icy experience called for the exercise of two gifts—*forethought,* they knew such a thing might happen and consequently laid up stores of food and fuel to meet it.

The other was *patience,* patience to endure day by day being absolutely cut off from the outside world, and patience to endure the severe cold.

Mr. Waye told me afterwards that he and his family were none the worse for it as they had plenty of food and fuel.

Many things are going to happen to us. We shall die, and in the great hereafter give an account of the stewardship of our earthly life to God. We shall see with unclouded vision the Glory of God. '' We shall see His Face.''

These coming events call for *forethought.* We must prepare to die. We must live a useful life of service, so that when we give the account of our stewardship, we may do it with joy and not with grief. We must also exercise *patience* to persevere to the end.

'' Keep yourselves in the Love of God and in the Patience of Christ.''

NATURE PROTECTS HERSELF.

OFTEN in the Spring of the year the heights of Dartmoor are wreathed in smoke from the swaler's fires, and at night the sky is illuminated with their glow. In very dry weather forest fires have been known to burn for days, but normally Nature protects herself in a very wonderful way.

Dartmoor has an unusually large range of day and night temperatures, and is liable to very heavy dews; these dews like a rain extinguish these fires.

Often have I watched a fire that has been burning furiously all day and the early part of the night, gradually flicker out towards midnight.

There is a copious dew which will protect us by extinguishing the destroying fires which spring up in a man's life—the copious dew of God's Grace.

Whether it is the fire of passion, or the fire of revenge, or the fire of hate, God's Grace will quench these destroying fires which flare up from the evil heart of man.

God has appointed His own *means* of Grace, and through these channels Grace must be sought—the study of God's Word, private prayer, public worship, regular reception of the Blessed Sacrament.

Are you devoutly using these? If not, why not?

What but God's Grace can foil the Tempter's power?—Nothing.

Then if we are faithful we must use them.—There is no reason why we should not.

OSMUNDA REGALIS.

COMMONLY called the King Fern. It grows luxuriantly in an environment which suits it, throwing out its giant fronds, but it requires a very moist climate and boggy peaty soil.

It has been nearly exterminated on Dartmoor, as townspeople, knowing nothing of its habits, but enamoured with its majestic form, tear it up by the roots and plant it in their town gardens—to languish and to die. This simple fact in Nature has its counterpart in the Spiritual world.

There is only one environment in which the soul of man can live and thrive—IN CHRIST.

" In whom we live and move and have our being."

The life of Christ is the native soil of the soul He has redeemed. His Life the atmosphere we breath, His love the warmth which strengthens our life, His gentleness that makes us great.

Yet men deliberately plant their soul in an environment in which it cannot grow—but must die.

There is no phrase in the New Testament more insisted upon than—IN CHRIST.

The most golden of all secrets of entering into this close union with our Saviour and perpetuating that union is becoming united with Him in the Blessed Sacrament.

" Whoso' eateth My Flesh and drinketh my Blood dwelleth in Me and I in him."

The supreme test of the depth of a man's Spiritual life is his attitude towards the Blessed Sacrament.

The careless Christian cares nothing for these things.

The man whose life is closely knit with Christ, hungers after the Bread of Life, and thirsts after the Blood of the Victorious Lamb.

> " Draw nigh and take the Body of the Lord
> And drink the Holy Blood for you outpoured."

ROUGH PATHS MY FEET HAVE TROD.

How true are these words of one who has had a long day—a 25 mile walk on Dartmoor.

Rough Paths—paths of all kinds, rabbit runs, sheep walks, cattle tracks, cart tracks, man's paths, grass trackways—and more often no path at all; stepping stones across a river, or only rough mossy wet boulders for a crossing and a difficult crossing it is. It is impossible to have a day across the Moor without some very rough ground.

Neither can we make our way through the world without crossing *some* rough ground. Owing to a mysterious dispensation of God's Providence some people have little else but rough ground to cross, and the path so rough that it is difficult to choose the way.

> " Thy way, not mine, O Lord
> However dark it be;
> Lead me by Thine own Hand
> Choose out the path for me."

Many a faithful servant of God can truthfully say as he draws nigh to his journey's end :

> " Rough paths my feet have trod
> Since first their course began.
> Feed me, Thou Bread of God,
> Help me, Thou Son of Man."

A GREEN PILLOW.

AT the source of many a stream is a large green pillow of beautiful moss which often covers a small but dangerous bog.

The Moss is filled with water. tread on it and down you go to investigate the Dartmoor underworld.

It has an unfortunate habit of forming a crust all round the edges in dry weather, which renders it dangerous to the inexperienced and the unwary.

Yet it looks so harmless, so attractive, so alluring.

Many things we meet with in life are the same.

If we are allured into them they will plunge us into the depths of ruin.

Here are a few :—I once saw the title of a sermon of a popular preacher to men, which gave three of these allurements in striking but vulgar terms

　　—the Pewter pot, the Petticoat and the Pony,

which expressed in ordinary terms are drink, women, and horse-racing.

Words of mine are not needed to explain either of these deadly perils which face men in this world; to some they are so alluring, so attractive, but they drown men in perdition, like the green bog draws the unwary traveller down into its watery embrace.

The Grace of our Lord Jesus Christ, and the Love of God and the Fellowship of the Holy Ghost equip men with power all sufficient to guard against and avoid these perils.

A RABBIT'S RUN.

In a delightful lane leading to Deancombe from Dean Churchtown there has long been a well used rabbit run, the rabbit track across the road has been worn quite smooth, but the track makes a striking curve.

The reason is the rabbits want to reach their holes on the far side of the road, and as the bank is too steep for them to climb into the holes, they make a circuitous route to avoid the steep of the bank, and so reach their holes.

What a simple lesson for us in overcoming the difficulties of life.

When you are faced with difficulties you can't overcome for the moment, don't give up the solution as hopeless—there is never a difficulty without a way out, difficulties are made to be overcome. Don't trust to yourself and your own powers. If the Holy Spirit of God is guiding your life, He will never fail to show you the way to overcome a difficulty if you seek His guidance.

The Holy Spirit desires to be your friend and show you the way; take His outstretched Hand and hold fast as long as life on earth lasts.

A RED BILLOWY SEA.

RARELY have I had such a walk as I had up the Avon
Valley on August 29th, 1929.   As we reached the
north end of Dockwell Ridge, and looked up the Avon
Valley it was a sea of heather.   On the N.E. spur of
Whittabarrow the colours and shadows were such as
I have seldom seen, further up the Valley as we passed
Bishop's Mead, on the slopes above, the heather was
as red as sliced beetroot.

On that unforgettable day we walked through mile
after mile of this beautiful heather, often up to one's
knees.   On one slope I found three large patches of
white heather.

What would that lovely landscape have been without
colour—little else but a dreary desert.

And what is our life without colour?

These are the heavenly colours which light up the
life of a good man, and make it so bright and gay.

The beauty of holiness, the splendour of purity, the
majesty of truth, the tenderness of love.   God grant
that our life may be adorned with these colours, and
so may we enjoy, even here on earth, a vision of the
heavenly life.

ROBIN REDBREAST.

THERE was a certain district in Brittany where no wheat had ever been grown, until one day a robin redbreast came from a far country with an ear of wheat in its beak which it dropped near a monastery. The monks picked it up and sowed the grains, and it produced a quantity of grains. Again and again they sowed the grains as they were produced, until the grains had multiplied sufficiently to enable the harvesters to reap enough corn to feed the whole of Brittany.

So little robin redbreast with its ear of wheat, which it dropped, became the means of feeding the whole land.

What may not *you* do, if you live a life devoted to our Saviour. The influence you may exercise by a word spoken, or a noble thought expressed, or by an act of Christian kindness, may spread far and wide.

As robin redbreast with its one ear of corn was the means of feeding the whole land, so you may become a power for good you little dream of.

Here will be the secret of your influence—your life lived *in Christ,* with Christ's example, with Christian principles and ideals.

What Florence Nightingale was to the Nursing profession, and Agnes Weston to the Sailors, and Elizabeth Fry was to the prisoners, you too in a degree may become in the sphere of work you take up in the Name of Jesus.

Remember Robin Redbreast.

FOOTPRINTS IN THE SAND.

AN Arab was once asked how he knew a man had crossed the desert. He answered—" By his footprints in the sand."

So Christ while on earth left his footprints in the sands, and by these we know he has been in this world.

On the sands of sin, sorrow, pain and danger Christ has left His footprints—He was sinless among sinners, a man of sorrows among the sorrowful, and He set His fearless foot amid the anguish of the World.

In some places the sands have shifted and His footprints are gone, but where the ground was firm they remain.

In Dartmoor streams where you see well shaped footprints in the sand it is safe to cross the stream.

Where Christ has trod and His footprints remain all is safe and He calls you on, and in the joy of His Presence the soul hears the glad sound of His Voice, and follows through this world—and then through tracts unknown.

We follow the Pioneer who leads us at last to the land we love, for like the Patriarchs of old

" We seek a country "

and we desire a better country, that is an heavenly.

A SILVER MOUNTAIN.

ON my way to Huntingdon Warren on March 5th, 1929, under the brilliant March sun the ice-cased snow covered the slopes of Whittabarrow Hill, above Bishop's Mead, shone with dazzling brightness like polished silver.

All this splendour was merely reflected light, dependent on the sun for its supply.

The blaze of light with which God's saints on earth shine and illuminate all around them is reflected light like this glazed ice reflected the light of the sun.

The saints live their lives in the Presence of Jesus the Very Light of the World, Whose Light lighteth every man that cometh into the world, Whose Truth penetrates the darkest places of the earth, Whose uprightness shines before men.

The lesson is simple.

" Let your light so shine before men that they may see your good works and glorify your Father which is in Heaven."

A SIMPLE DUTY ALWAYS BLEST.

A HUNDRED yards east of Sheepstor Church is a cottage, here for many years lived a faithful man and his invalid wife, and a daughter afflicted with St. Vitus dance who lived on the floor; nothing that was done seemed to improve her, but she rather grew worse—she is gone now.

On the happy day Bishop Robertson dedicated the Rood Screen, he confirmed the mother and daughter in their home.

After their Confirmation, for 5 years till they left the parish, I always reserved the Blessed Sacrament at the 8 o'clock Service on the 1st Sunday of each month, and immediately after the Service I walked from the Church fully robed bearing the Blessed Sacrament to their home and then communicated them.

Sheepstor is one of the wettest places in England and very subject to intensive rainstorms.

On those journeys during those 5 years never once did rain fall on me; many times have I known the rain to stop on a stormy morning while I went there in the dry—many a rough wild rainy night was followed by a calm fine morning.

In that 5 years only once did preciptation fall on me, and then the air was full of snowflakes on a very snowy morning, and my little journey was through a veritable fairy land.

The immunity from storm and flood in doing this simple duty each month made a great impression on my life—never to be forgotten.

I always felt that God approved my reserving the Sacrament, and was well pleased with my doing that simple duty each month, to have protected me so lovingly through those five years.

I felt God used to lead the way.

> " Thy way is in the storm and Thy path in the great waters and Thy footsteps are not known."

SNOW SHOWERS.

THE Metaphor of Snow Showers is a very favourite one with St. Chrysostom to describe troubles that come upon man.

Snow showers are common on Dartmoor, but seldom seen there to perfection, as they are in the E. and S.E. of England.

I will describe one.

The day is nearly cloudless and the sun warm, suddenly with hardly any warning the sky is filled with whirling snow like smoke, driven with a fierce wind; then there is semi-darkness and the air is filled with blinding snow like fog.

As the storm passes the snow becomes less, then all passes and the sun comes out and all is a fairy land with the deep snow.

These follow in succession at intervals during the day.

St. Chrysostom was right when he compared troubles to snow showers.

(1) There is the suddenness with which they come on without the least warning.

(2) Life becomes dark, it is as tho' the sun had gone out, and life seems so dreary and sad, everything seems dark.

(3) When the storm is passing the light gradually returns.

(4) If the storm has been bravely faced and weathered, after it has passed, in spiritual values a fairyland is left—" We are nearer my God to Thee," we have grown in grace and strength.

(5) When the storms of life's little day are over, no more storms to come, but breathless calm; the scene beautiful beyond imagination, and all illuminated with the soft warm rays of the Glory of God and the Light of the Lamb.

A   CLASSIC   SNOW   SQUALL.

A CLASSIC example of the kind of storm St. Chryostom describes to illustrate troubles was what is known as the Eurydice Storm which swept across the South of England late in the afternoon on March 24th, 1878.

One fine hot March day the storm came on without any warning, and in half an hour the snow lay deep on the ground.

The training ship *Eurydice,* which had been stationed in the West Indies 3 or 4 years, filled with young boys now in sight of home as they neared Dunnose Head off Ventnor.   The storm struck the ship, the sails became plastered with snow when a violent squall capsized her and over 300 boys were drowned.

I remember it as the most tragic instance of sorrow in my early childhood—300 mothers mourning the loss of their sons.

This great disaster had a small cause, so also has many a trouble in life, but the consequences are appalling.

As we make our voyage across the sea of the world with the great uncertainty and dangers of the voyage, may God in His love and mercy spare us troubles, except those He sees to be needful for us.   Be friends with the Great Helmsman and

> " Come to thy God in time,
> Thus saith the ocean chime.
> Storm, billow, whirlwind past
> Come to thy God at last.''

A PATH THROUGH THE SNOW FOR THE FAITHFUL.

In my Weather Journal on Christmas Day, 1918, I find this note : —

    " I swept the snow off the Church path for my Christmas Communicants to come in with dry boots."

ON several occasions on a winter's morning, mine has been the joy to sweep a path through the snow for my early Communicants, so that they may enter the Church with their boots clear of snow, and so avoid kneeling through the Service with cold wet boots with snow clinging to them.

Occasions of this indelibly impressed on my mind are Christmas morning, 1918, when the ground was covered with snow at Sheepstor, and I swept a path clean and dry through the snow for my Christmas Communicants.

Another occasion in February, 1917; when the snow was several inches deep, and I had a formidable task to cut a path with a shovel, and how hot I became.

On the Feast of the Epiphany 1920 at Dean, I had the same joy.

The Lesson of this simple friendly action is always to do what you can to help and encourage the Faithful in their life of Service to God. " Serving the Lord " is difficult enough, how pleasant and encouraging it is to feel that others are interested and trying to help you.

Never lose an opportunity of helping and encouraging one of Christ's own to draw nearer to Him. Discomfort in doing so ought never to be thought of. This is the simple lesson of a clean path cut through the snow on a Church path on a winter's morning.

SON OF THE CLOUD.

THIS was the name the later Jews gave Jesus Christ and the reason was this : —

Of his Second Coming to Earth it was foretold.

" Behold He cometh with clouds and every eye shall see Him."

The idea is that when He comes that He will not simply be surrounded by clouds, but that He will compel the clouds into His retinue.

The Psalmist says : " God maketh the clouds His chariots and walketh upon the wings of the wind."

In the vast retinue of angels and the redeemed which will follow the Lamb at his coming will be the clouds.

When you see the clouds trailing across the Dartmoor heights, think of this—at the day of Christ's Coming the clouds will be seen, not trailing driven by the winds, but drawn along by Christ in His retinue, *not* as dark angry clouds, but all aglow with the dazzling glory with which He will illuminate the world.

A SOUTH ASPECT.

A VIXEN will usually choose for her cubs an earth whose entrance faces south; she will often lay her litter in a badger's earth, choosing one that faces the sun, in whose rays the cubs like to bask and to frolic and frisk in their youthful games.

As you live your life, always choose a sunny aspect —in the Presence of our Lord, the Very Light of the World, Whose glory will illuminate all the deep recesses of your life, as time goes on, and your life will be warmed and strengthened with the sunshine of His Love—the Love of Christ, which passeth knowledge.

A DARTMOOR SUNSET.

THERE is no finer place in England to see a grand sunset than the Western heights of Dartmoor.

There is the beautiful country in the foreground flooded with the golden light of the setting sun; in the background silhouetted against the clear sky are the Cornish heights as black as soot.

Above the setting sun, extending to the zenith and beyond, are the crimson and blood red clouds of indescribable grandeur. Concentrate your vision on the clouds and they become to you like rays of glory from another world—a reflection of the Glory of God.

" The heavens declare the Glory of God."

Grand sunsets, tho' only natural phenomena are to me the first rays and the pledge of the ineffable glory THE GLORY will manifest to us in the next world.

Coming events cast their shadows before them, so the advancing Glory flashes His rays in advance of His path. Our dear Lord THE GLORY† is the shining light that shineth more and more unto the Perfect Day.

† S. James II. 1, R.V.

THISTLEDOWN.

OFTEN have I watched thistledown drifting along on the wind. Some fall near one's feet, others caught by a sudden breeze suddenly rise, clear the hedge and pass on—whither one cannot say.

Thistledown will travel like this for miles and sow thistles wherever it eventually comes to earth.

The thistle in the Old Testament is the symbol of sin.

Does not thistledown travelling on the wind remind us that evil is spread in the same way.

One never knows where the thistledown will finally alight.

So if you speak an evil word, you never know how far it will carry.

One evil action done, the consequences will spread far and wide, and like the travelling thistledown you never know how far it will travel and how much evil will be sown.

If you wantonly do evil, God will bring home to you some day what you have done, and how far the seeds of evil you have sown have scattered.

A TINKLING STREAMLET.

WHAT is more soothing to the ear than running water. What more cheering to the heart of man than the tinkling streamlet as it flows through a lonely valley, up in the Dartmoor Highlands, with its heather-clad slopes.

In such the little streamlet merrily tinkling on its course is the only companion one has; often no human being within miles and not an animal of any kind in sight.

The tinkling streamlet with its waters so clear and pure, with its merry laughter as it tinkles onward along its course, often the only companion of the Dartmoor wanderer in an upland valley.

This clear, limpid rill speaks to us of the purity of the life Jesus gives to each soul that lives in Him.

The clearness of its living water tells of the transparent honesty of the life that is hid with Christ in God.

The merry laughter as it tinkles along its way, which not even obstacles can silence, teaches us the true happiness of the life in Christ—that true joy of the Lord which is the strength of the loyal child of God.

No matter what obstacles or difficulties beset our path, this joy no man takes from us—

> " Joy past all speech, of glory full
> But stored where none may know
> As Manna hid in dewy heaven
> As pearls in ocean low.''

GREEN TRACKWAYS.

No visitor to Dartmoor can have failed to notice how the Moor is intersected by green trackways. Nothing grows on these trackways except the delightful green turf of the finest texture with its green grass.

No furze, no heather, no whorts scrub can find root there.

Each of these trackways leads somewhere.

We have to make our journey along the pathway of life. Let us see to it that no rank growths spring up in our path and spoil the way.

Sin, bad habits, slackness.

These have a way of springing up in our path.

Not one of these can grow in our path if we pursue the right way—Christ the Way. In Him is no sin, in Him no imperfections.

A TRAGEDY OF THE STORM.

OUTSIDE Huntingdon Warren House three weeks after
the great snow of February, 1929, I saw the head of
a guinea fowl peeping out of the melting snow; it had
been overwhelmed and buried in the snowstorm and
had been suffocated.

As I saw that unfortunate bird with its body frozen
stiff, with its head peeping out of the snow, I thought
how often a man dies and no one cares.

I have on several occasions buried a poor man
without a single mourner—

> " Rattle his bones over the stones,
>   He's only a pauper whom nobody owns."

But tho' the world is cold, cheerless and
unsympathetic, Jesus told us we have a Father in
Heaven who cares, and not even a sparrow falls to the
ground without His knowledge.

At those funerals I took without a mourner, I often
felt that One Mourner was present there whom we
could not see, Who tho' unseen, unheard, soon made
His Presence felt the moment the Funeral began,
when the silence was broken by those ringing words
of hope and peace.

> " I am the Resurrection and the Life saith the Lord."

Our one Mourner was Jesus, the Victor of the
Grave.

WHERE THE WILD ASSES QUENCH THEIR THIRST.

BETWEEN Western Beacon and Butterdon Hill on the lowest ground between the two hills is Black Pool. Here all kinds of animals come and drink.

The Pool does not look an inviting place to quench the thirst. Its name describes it—the water looks as black as jet, stained with the black peat as it fills a natural shallow basin in the peat soil.

There is one of nature's lessons to be learnt from these animals—they come and drink *after* they have finished their meal.

Men eat and drink at the same time, hence they develop digestive disorders and similar complaints.

Here is a simple law of health for us.

Eat first, drink afterwards.

WITHERED GRASS.

During the Autumn and Winter the Moor is in most places covered with a long coarse grass which gives it rather a dreary appearance.

In the mellow sunlight of an Autumn day it is a beautiful fawn colour.

The withered grass reminds us of the cry of the prophet : —

" All flesh is as grass and all the goodliness thereof is as the flower of the field : the grass withereth, the flower fadeth : because the Spirit of the Lord bloweth upon it; surely the people is grass. The grass withereth, the flower fadeth : but the Word of our God shall stand for ever."

In mankind generation followeth generation; one generation soon passeth, but the Word of God abides.

The withered grass impresses us with the lesson of the transitoriness of man's life on the earth—which to-day is and to-morrow is not.

INDEXES.

PART 1.

	PAGE
Ammil	18
Beardown Man	6
Bee, the Honey	21
Bird, the Demon	7
Bullocks, Scotch	34
Bowerman's Nose	9
Broom, Golden	10
Cloud Shadows	11
Cross shows the way, The	12
Cut Lane	13
Dawn, a high	20
Death, not divided, In	14
Ephraim's Pinch	15
Flaxen Hair	16
Footprints of the Morning	17
Game, Black	8
Glory, a ray of	29
Glory, Rosy	31
Glory, a scene of Unimaginable	18
Hawk and its prey	19
Heather, White	5
Ice Grotto	22
Lark with its Morning Song	23
Mouse, the Field	24
Patchwork Pattern	26
Peat Fires	27
Preface	3
Purple and Gold	28
Ringleshutts	30
Sacrifice, a Pagan	32
Salmon, cheap	33
Scents, Sweet	46
Sea of Glass	35
Shelter, place of	36
Snow, an Altar Cloth of	37
Snow Cornice	38
Snow Dam	39
Snow, Drifting	40
Snow Fountain	41
Snow Tunnel	42
Snow, Virgin	43
Stepping Stones	44
Sunrise, a Red	45
Taken, One	25
Windstrew, The	47

PART 2.

	PAGE
Boys, Three	7
Cala Rag, Whetlow	8
Chicken Scratching	9
Converging paths	10
Crosses along the way	11
Crystal Streams	5
Crystal Streams in action	6
Curiosity	12
Deserted road, a	13
Fires, between three	14
Forest Fires	15
Gingaford	16
Golden West	18
Grave, a chief's	17
Grave, a lonely	20
Icy Spring, an	19
Index	47
Mists	21
Moss, luminous	22
Moss on boulders	23
Noah	24
Nature protects herself	25
Osmunda	26
Paths, rough	27
Pillow, a green	28
Rabbits' run	29
Red Sea, a	30
Robin redbreast	31
Sand, Footprints in	32
Silver Mountain, a	33
Simple duty, a	34
Snow Showers	35
Snow Shower, a classic	36
Snow path	37
Son of the Cloud	38
South Aspect, a	39
Sunset, a Dartmoor	40
Thistledown	41
Tinkling Streamlet, a	42
Trackways	43
Tragedy, a	44
Wild asses	45
Withered Grass	46

JOHN KEBLE from the Summit of Plynlimon wrote :

Go up and watch the new-born rill
 Just trickling from its mossy bed,
Streaking the heath-clad hill
 With a bright emerald thread.

Can'st thou her bold career foretell
 What rocks she shall o'erleap or rend,
How far in ocean's swell
 Her freshening billows send?

. . . . . .

Even so, the course of prayer who knows?
 It springs in silence where it will,
Springs out of sight and flows
 At first a lonely rill.

But streams shall meet it by and by
 From thousand sympathetic hearts,
Together swelling high
 Their chant of many parts.

A NEW DARTMOOR SERIES.

THE DARTMOOR FOREST SERIES.

No. 1. Ready 1930. **Dartmoor Forest.**—South.

No. 2. Ready 1931. **Dartmoor Forest.**—West.

No. 3.

No. 4. **The Heart of Dartmoor.**   Price 1/6.   Post 2d.
   (North-East and Centre).   **Now Ready.**

No. 5. **A Dartmoor Snowstorm.**   Price 1/6.   Post 2d.
  (The Great Blizzard of Christmas, 1927).   **Now Ready.**

No. 6. **A Great Winter on Dartmoor** (1928–29)—with accounts of the unprecedented snowstorm at Dean Prior of February 16th, 1929, and the Great Ice Storm of the closing days of February.
   Ready Easter, 1930.   Price 1/-.   Post 1½d.

A NEW SERIES.

THE WORD PICTURES OF THE BIBLE.
     In Parts, 1/- each.   Post 1½d.
Being a Collection of the Metaphors and Similies of the Bible with their Lessons.

New Testament, Part 1.   " Some Aspects of Life."
     Now Ready.   Price 1/-.   Post 1½d.

Part 2.   " Personal Religion."   **Now Ready.**

Part 3.   " Life after Death."

Part 4.   " Some Picturesque Scenes in the New Testament."
    In preparation.

Part 5.   " Some Lessons from Bird and Animal Life in the New Testament."   Ready Advent, 1930.

A NEW SERIES.

THE SPIRITUAL LESSONS FROM NATURE SERIES.

No. 1. **Spiritual Lessons from Dartmoor Forest.**
  Part 1.   " White Heather " and other Studies.
    Now Ready.   Price 1/-.   Post 1½d.
  Part 2.   " Crystal Streams " and other studies.
    Now Ready.   Price 1/-.   Post 1½d.
  Part 3.   " Granite Chips."

Appendices

APPENDIX I

BOOKS WRITTEN AND PUBLISHED BY THE REVEREND H. HUGH BRETON, M.A.

THE BEAUTIFUL DARTMOOR SERIES
(Originally called THE SHEEPSTOR SERIES):

1911   *Part 1:   Sheepstor and Its Border Lands.
1912   *Part 2:   The Northern Quarter of the Moor.
1913   *Part 3:   The Southern Quarter of the Moor.
1912   Part 4:   The Breezy Cornish Moors.
1912   Part 5:   Lands End and The Lizard.

(Parts 1 to 3 were also entitled Beautiful Dartmoor and Its Interesting Antiquities.)

THE MORWENSTOW SERIES OF SHILLING BOOKS:

1926   No. 1:   Morwenstow.
1926   No. 2:   The North Coast of Cornwall.
1926   No. 3:   Hawker of Morwenstow.
1926   No. 4:   The Heart of Dartmoor.

1928   The Great Blizzard of Christmas, 1927.
1929   *Spiritual Lessons from Dartmoor Forest
      (Part 1. "White Heather" and other studies)
      The Word Pictures of The Bible
      (New Testament, Part 1 "Some Aspects of Life").
1930   The Great Winter of 1928–29
      *Spiritual Lessons from Dartmoor Forest
      (Part 2. "Crystal Streams" and other studies)
      The Word Pictures of The Bible
      (New Testament, Part 2 "Personal Religion")
1931   *The Forest of Dartmoor (Part 1—South-East).
1932   *The Forest of Dartmoor (Part 2—South-West).

*Republished in facsimile edition 1990.

APPENDIX II

PROJECTED BOOKS BY THE REVEREND H. HUGH BRETON, M.A. NOT PUBLISHED

The Forest of Dartmoor (Part 3: North-West).
The Forest of Dartmoor (Part 4: North-East).

THE SPIRITUAL LESSONS FROM NATURE SERIES:

No. 1:   Spiritual Lessons from Dartmoor Forest:
         Part 3: Granite Chips in a Granite Country.
         (Parts 1 and 2 were "White Heather" and "Crystal
         Streams" as listed in Appendix I)
No. 2:   Spiritual Lessons from the Cornish Sea.
No. 3:   Spiritual Lessons from the Cornish Mountains.

THE WORD PICTURES OF THE BIBLE:

New Testament, Part 3:   "Life after Death".
                Part 4:   "Our Daily Life in God's Presence".
                Part 5:   "Some Picturesque Scenes in the
                New Testament".
                Part 6:   "Some Lessons from Bird and Animal
                Life in the New Testament".

Robert Furze, Gentleman

APPENDIX III

BOOKS WRITTEN BY MIKE LANG

Grand Prix! Volume 1—1950 to 1965
Grand Prix! Volume 2—1966 to 1973
Grand Prix! Volume 3—1974 to 1980
Grand Prix! The Grand Prix! Trilogy—1950 to 1980
*Grand Prix! Volume 4—1981 to 1984

(Each sub-titled Race-by-Race account of Formula 1 World
Championship motor racing and published by Haynes Publishing
Group PLC, Sparkford, Nr Yeovil, Somerset BA22 7JJ).

*Due to be published shortly.